Hegarty on Creativity

Thames & Hudson

there

Are

e.s.

Introduction: On Creativity

Feel like writing the next hit song, painting another *Mona Lisa*, or becoming the next Tarantino? If the answer to any of these questions is yes – or if you can easily substitute in your own creative goals and still say yes – then you can bet that understanding the creative process is going to be crucial to your success.

Creativity touches all our lives in a thousand different ways, from the clothes we buy to the buildings we live in, from the food we eat to the cars we drive. Creativity invents, perfects, and defines our world. It explains and entertains us.

Almost every facet of our lives is influenced by it. And its impact is only getting stronger as time goes on. It's not surprising then that we're always being told the future is creative!

But what drives creativity? Inspires it? Sustains it?

I've spent the past forty years pursuing a creative career in advertising. In this time, I've had the privilege of working with some of the best creative minds out there – filmmakers, musicians, writers, illustrators, photographers, and designers.

In my experience, very few people have a clear idea of what is meant by creativity or what it means to be creative. No, it's not an excuse to grow your hair long, wear weird clothes, and be rude to people. You may wish to do all those things, but that won't make you a better creative person. But being aware, sensitive, passionate, concerned, committed, and above all inventive just might – these are the necessary ingredients to a successful creative career.

There are many ways of defining creativity but the one I like best is 'the expression of self.' It's a definition that captures my belief that we're *all* creative – though naturally some are better at it than others.

The creative process is about inputs not outtakes. This book's about how you get started, how you keep going. Not what you want to create. You'll have to decide that.

We're all creative but only some of us will be lucky enough to earn our living by it. Interested in being one of these lucky few?
Read on.

Here are fifty provocations on creativity – on nurturing it, sustaining it, and harnessing it. But remember, there are no rules, only guidelines. Infuriating, isn't it?

By the way, if you're holding the special edition of this book, you can eat it. Flip to page 126 for further details.

Now that's useful.

John Hegarty

The Blank Page

The blank page is one of the greatest challenges faced by the creative person.

Writers often talk about the fear that overcomes them when they first put that blank page into the typewriter and wonder what they're going to write. Whether it's a blank screen, a blank canvas, or the blank page of a sketchbook, the effect is the same. Creativity is the creation of something out of nothing and that can be scary. However, from that blank canvas might appear a painting that will capture the viewer's imagination, propelling them into another time and place. David Hockney's *A Bigger Splash* does exactly that for me.

But how to start? How to overcome feelings of possible inadequacy, fears of failure? Woody Allen has often said he *Loves* **the process of writing; he can't wait to get started. So what's the secret?**

I suppose it's the conviction that there is no such thing as failure. Rejecting the possibility of failure is the first step. When you're creating something from nothing – a painting, a novel, a movie script – the fear of failure is always there. This will compromise your idea. You have to be supremely confident in your ability to achieve something outstanding.

If confidence is one key to success, enjoying your work is another. Even more than confidence, the sense of excitement that accompanies being creative will spur you on. Just think of it as playing – you can do anything you want, go anywhere you like.

And that blank canvas doesn't have to start blank – I mean, figuratively, not literally. Start small with some sketches. Likewise, a whole novel isn't in your head before you start to write. A plot maybe, a character. Well, write those down and gradually a picture will emerge, the story will begin to unfold.

The very process of sketching, writing, whatever, this process will help you explain your idea – *to yourself*.

Start small, start compact, and suddenly you'll have begun to create.

And then you're no longer looking at a blank page.

Ideas

Every day we have ideas. They are the most profound of products that we as humans generate.

> Big ones, silly ones, funny ones – the irreverent to the groundbreaking. Ideas are the driving force of human progress. From the discovery of the wheel to the internal combustion engine, for better or worse ideas are mankind's contribution to our planet's development. Some are good and sadly some are bad. Like peanut butter. Disgusting stuff.

And, of course, ideas are the building blocks of creativity. Whatever you create, from writing to filmmaking to painting to composing, you start with an idea. Without one, you have nothing.

> An idea can be defined as 'a thought or plan formed by mental effort.' I particularly like that phrase 'mental effort.' It implies you've done something of substance. And that's what interests me: Ideas of substance. Not whether you should go for pizza tonight as opposed to sushi. As ideas go, coming up with an answer to that might resolve the immediate question but it isn't exactly going to get you headlines around the world. And surely that's what *we* want to do. We're after

 ideas.

YOU CAN HAVE IDEAS ANYWHERE!

It's important to add that having ideas is the most democratic of all the activities that we undertake. You don't need special permission or a certificate to come up with a good idea. This can be done anywhere, at any time, without any special equipment or prior practice. It can be done sitting down, standing up, or lying down. Indeed, often the right idea will come to you when you're not even thinking. That's how brilliant we are at generating ideas, whatever our race, creed, color, gender, or age. Ideas are always there for you, waiting for you to think them up.

And if your idea is profound enough, it could change the course of history.

Not bad, is it?

So let's remember to celebrate our freedom and ability to conjure ideas from nowhere. Just make sure you share them with the world.

ORIGINAL IS DEPEN UPON THE YOUR SO

ITY

DENT

OF

OK, let's get it out of the way.
There is no such thing as originality.

URCES.

'Original' is one of the most inflammatory words a creative person can use to describe a creative work, 'fake,' of course, being the other. It's also one of the most meaningless words in the creative lexicon. By definition, nothing can be truly original.

It is said that God was the last originator and the rest of us are just copyists. And the truth is that everything we create is based on something that's gone before. It has to be. Nothing happens in a vacuum, least of all creativity and ideas.

Ideas borrow, blend, subvert, develop, and bounce off other ideas.

So it's an arrogance to say your idea is original. In fact, the value of an idea is in how it draws its inspiration from the world around us and then reinterprets it in a way we haven't seen before.

Being different and daring is important, but original?
No.

Now blatantly stealing someone else's idea is wrong. But thinking that your idea is original is also wrong. Your idea only exists in relation to another idea. We all stand on each other's shoulders and in doing so hopefully see further.

A cynic would say that originality is dependent upon the obscurity of your sources. But as you'll learn on page 51, I don't like cynics.

So rather than original I use a much better word:

FRESH

Creativity has to question, explain, and inspire our view of the world, so when reaching for freshness ask yourself these questions:

Does this piece of creative work stop you? Would you notice it straight away? It's not for nothing that we say no one ever bought anything while they were asleep.

Does this work make you look at an issue in a different way? Does it awaken your interest in the subject, leading you to reassess your opinion of it?

Has the work and its process of creation made you understand the world in a different, more moving, inspiring, or thoughtful way? Does it move you to action?

These questions will take you to the heart of the matter. Getting to the point when you can answer yes to all of them is the difficult bit.

Fearlessness

A researcher at our advertising agency once asked me a seemingly simple yet very complex question:

What does it take to be creative?

I replied that we are all creative and that's what makes humans so interesting: We all come up with ideas. Question answered.

Or so I thought, until my colleague responded:

*But you earn your living by it, so what do **you** have that makes that possible?*

I was a little taken aback by this reply as I hadn't really considered that side of things before. I live by instinct and instinct has always driven me to follow my creative beliefs. But that's not much of an answer.

So I took a step back and thought about what I've done and what I admire most about what other people have done, and I realized that there is one thing I value above all else.

What does it take to be creative?

Fearlessness.

Not quite what I had in mind Fanshaw when I said we need to be more DARING!

You have to have the ability to pursue and present an idea that is genuinely fresh, that is as different as you can possibly make it. You have to put your creative reputation on the line.

Fearlessness is essential in the advertising industry where you have to arrive in the office with a new idea and pitch it to a bunch of skeptics. Every day. In fact, it's essential in every creative profession. I'm sure that when Danny Boyle proposed his idea for the opening ceremony of the London 2012 Olympics, a whole chorus of voices doubted him:

British history?

We haven't seen that before...

Are you sure that will work?

That doesn't look very sporty...

But Boyle believed in his vision and he was fearless in pursuing what he thought the opening ceremony could and should be. The result was brilliant and fresh and will forever change the way others strive to stage ceremonies that will surprise and delight in equal measure.

What's the point in producing something that follows a formula?

None.

What does it take to produce something that doesn't?

Fearlessness.

Chaos vs. Process

START.

Creating a workplace culture in which creativity can flourish is never easy and much has been written about how best to do this.

Essentially, there are two schools of thought: Chaos and process.

The chaos theory is one followed by many creative companies:

Have very little structure and foster an atmosphere of mild mayhem, an atmosphere in which ideas get thrown around and timetables largely ignored. That is, until panic sets in and results have to be produced. Eventually out of this freewheeling, unencumbered atmosphere, greatness will emerge.

Or so you hope.

Anyone who has seen the documentary on the making of The Rolling Stones album *Exile on Main Street* will understand what I mean by creative chaos.

For many people chaos will be scary.
Undisciplined and unpredictable.

The other possibility is to introduce process.
To implement systems that should ensure the smooth development of an idea and to schedule in time for the creative work to be nurtured. People talk about processes liberating creativity.

If you're running a creative company, it's up to you to decide which approach you favor. Chaos can be exactly that and result in nothing usable. But equally process can be dangerous because instead of liberating creativity it restricts it.

In the end, you have to decide what your nerves can take and how much sleep you want at night.

No wonder corporate companies view creativity with such suspicion.

FINISH.

We're All Artists

Yes, we're all artists.
But some of us shouldn't exhibit.

These wise words should be seared into all our psyches. And anyone who doubts them should be made to visit the Sunday art fair on the railings separating London's Green Park and Piccadilly...
(Spoiler alert: It's all terrible.)

Of course, being creative is a natural state for humans, but some of us are definitely better at it than others.

For example, we can all dance – there's no doubt about that – but some of us have the wisdom to sit out during those moments when the dance floor beckons.

Now I know this might be the most obvious thing in the world to state, but sadly we live in a world where increasingly everybody thinks they can do everything. And that they should inflict it on everyone else.

GARRET TO LET
Uncomfortable, cold in winter, hot in summer. Noisy. Inaccessible. Poor Ventilation. Cheap. Perfect for artist.

Well the answer is no, you shouldn't.

Just because technology has made it easier to create and express yourself does not mean you're any good at it. Every day I'm inundated with badly written, poorly constructed, uninformed blogs.

Please.

STOP

Do us all a favor and find something useful to do.

One of the great skills in life is to recognize talent and respect it. Recognize your own and you'll learn more and feel far more satisfied.

'Despite appearances I'm incredibly complex, sensitive and prone to prolonged bouts of introspection.'

Simple Truths

Whatever you're creating, simplicity is the ultimate goal. The power of reduction, as we say in advertising, means taking a complex thought and reducing it down to a simple, powerful message.

From a painting to a novel to a movie, there is only one space you want to fill. And that's the space between someone's ears. Your tool of persuasion might be a paintbrush or a guitar, but it's your audience's mind that you really want. Once you've captured a corner of that, you'll have made it.

But if your idea or message is too complicated it will bewilder and confuse your audience. Even in business they say complexity destroys profitability. (Though make sure you don't trivialize your idea either. If that happens, what you're saying won't stick.)

How then to create something that has the power to stay in someone's mind *and* capture their imagination?

At the foundation of any great idea is the truth, the most powerful force in creativity.

Just think of any great work, regardless of medium. It is almost certainly expressing a distinct point of view. But if that point of view doesn't contain a truth, then you can bet that the work's impact will be fleeting.

And so it is that anyone who wants to create has to find their voice, their truth. At its most basic level, if you don't believe in what you're doing, why should anyone else?

Finding your own truth and expressing it imaginatively is the skill you must develop, and very often keeping it simple will show you the way.

Blaise Pascal, the great French philosopher, summed it up well when writing to a friend. He concluded his letter: 'My apologies for this letter being so long. Had I more time it would have been shorter.'

So whether you're writing, painting, acting, directing, or designing, the truth simply expressed is the difference between that piece of work being meaningful or meaningless.

You might achieve momentary success by ignoring this fact but it won't endure. And, furthermore, you won't get satisfaction from it.

No one creates just for the sake of creating. We create to make a point. To express an attitude, a belief. Even if, like me, you work in advertising.

The greatest strategy you can employ is the truth. It is handy also, because you can always remember what you've said.

Head vs. Heart

Stop thinking.

Start feeling.

Creativity is an intellectual process, but it is also one driven by the heart. Irish writer James Stephens summed it up perfectly when he wrote:

What the heart knows today, the head will understand tomorrow.

As humans, we respond more to emotions than we do to logic. Anyone who doubts this should try and explain why people go on smoking, despite the warning sign on every pack that reads:

SMOKING KILLS

Fashion is another example of this reality. It's an industry driven almost entirely by emotion. How something looks and feels, how it stimulates the senses, is much more important than its function. To make this point all I have to say is high-heel shoes. If they're Louboutins that makes my point even more persuasive.

BOXING

IN BOARDROOMS EVERYWHERE

Under the Promotion of Millward Brown

EVERY WEEK

SAM

BERT

HEART vs HEAD

SPECIAL 8 ROUNDS OR A KNOCKOUT

WITH LINK TEST SUBJECT TO

CONSUMER FEEDBACK

SPECIAL FOCUS GROUP SEATING

RINGSIDE & STAGE

ALL SEATS RESERVED

It's equally important that as creators we let go too and see where our work takes us. Over rationalizing what you're doing will endanger its potential. Now this doesn't mean you should hide from identifying a purpose to underpin your creativity, but it should encourage you to listen to your heart and let your emotions guide you. If you've ever seen a documentary on Jackson Pollock, you will absolutely understand the importance of this. Not for him the premeditated, preplanned work of art.

When I'm asked, *When do you do your best thinking?* My answer is always, *When I'm not thinking.*

That's why a brainstorming session is a complete and utter waste of time for the truly creative person. The idea that, say at ten o'clock on Thursday morning, you can attend a meeting and suddenly be creative is ridiculous. Creativity doesn't work like that.

Too much thinking jeopardizes the creative process, slowing or stopping altogether your imagination and emotions from exploring every possibility out there. And exploration is essential to being creative. Knowing where you're going to end up is fine when mountain climbing but it's no good when you're in the process of creating, hopefully, a masterpiece. Could this be why we feel accountancy is the opposite of creativity?

Get Angry

When Picasso painted *Guernica*, one of his most famous works, I don't think he was whistling happily to himself. No, he was angry. Outraged at the Nazis and Italian Fascists who had bombed this defenseless Spanish town, killing thousands of innocent people.

For most of us, anger amounts to stress, and the worst type of stress at that. But for artists, anger can be a positive force. If focused and channeled into a piece of work, it is capable of producing something of great profundity.

When you are intent on putting a great wrong right, creativity will often exceed all expectations. Out of conflict comes purpose.

Take Charles Dickens as another example. He devoted himself to chronicling the terrible injustices of his day in his novels. Do you think *he* was whistling happily away when he wrote *A Christmas Carol*? I don't. The opening line of that book is 'Marley was dead.' It's not exactly the light-hearted tone of 'I'm dreaming of a white Christmas.'

Years ago I was working on an anti-smoking campaign and feeling upset at the idea that secondary smoke was harming children. The poster I helped to create featured a toddler smoking a cigarette under the headline, 'How many cigarettes a day does your child smoke?' It was hugely effective in raising awareness and changing behavior. Being angry made it happen.

So get angry but don't let it eat you up. Instead, find a piece of paper, a canvas, anything, and get it out of you. You'll be amazed at how therapeutic this can be. And how creative.

Words Are a Barrier to Communication

There's no question about it. We live in a visual culture increasingly dominated by screens. From your smart TV to your iPhone to your iPad, we're seeing more but reading less. All courtesy of digital technology.

With so many screens and so much information out there, we've had to find a way of absorbing it more effectively. Hence the value of visual language has increased, even as the influence of the written word has decreased.

Whether you deem this change a catastrophe or not, you and every other creative person out there still have to grapple with the realities that exist. For the writer, the rise of the visual could be considered a major problem *or* a brilliant opportunity. You see, the power of reduction has come into play, so ask yourself:

Can I edit my message down into a shorter, more distinct phrase?

Can I spark your imagination with even fewer words?

Some of us might say that the pithy phrase is only a sound bite and how tragic that we've been reduced to a world of sound bites. Well, I think we have always lived in such a world. If the French Revolution and the aspirations of its revolutionaries could be reduced to 'Liberté, Égalité, Fraternité,' then surely whatever it is that you're trying to communicate can also be edited down.

If it's a race to get into minds and stay there, then it's the artists who make their points faster, smarter, and more thought-provoking that will be the ones to succeed.

Juxtaposition

Juxtaposition is the art of placing together a number of contrasting objects or ideas, usually two. Used effectively, it captures our imaginations immediately, making it one of the most valuable techniques any creator can employ to dramatize their message. And it's at its most potent when these two objects are as diametrically opposed to each other as possible.

I remember learning that when painting if you want to make black seem even blacker then you juxtapose it with white. It is as simple as that. So many artists have used this technique to add drama to their works. René Magritte's *Empire of Light***, for example, shows an illuminated street at night, yet the blue sky above it belongs to a sunny day. That juxtaposition of night and day makes the picture.**

The world of fashion also loves using juxtaposition, even down to describing trends: 'Blue is the new black.' The Beatles sang, 'It's been a hard day's night,' and so created one of their greatest hits. Indeed, many rock bands employ juxtaposition when coming up with a memorable name. Curved Air, Soft Machine, Atomic Kitten are just some of those that come to mind. Comedy also loves a bit of incongruous juxtaposition – think of Monty Python's philosophers-versus-poets football match or lumberjacks singing about women's underwear.

Juxtaposition is employed in every possible creative field, always sharpening our response and reaction to an idea. By placing two things next to one another that wouldn't normally sit together we force our minds to resolve this apparent conundrum. And it's in provoking that simple process that an idea really begins to stick.

Zag

It's amazing what you can learn from a black sheep.

> One of our first clients at BBH was Levi Strauss. It was 1982 and the company wanted to launch a campaign for black denim but needed the right idea to communicate.

We came up with this poster.

When we presented it to the client for the first time,
they were horrified.

Where's the picture of the jeans?! they exclaimed.

BLACK LEVI'S.
WHEN THE WORLD ZIGS, ZAG.

I responded by pointing out to them politely – well, relatively politely... – that everyone knows what a pair of jeans looks like and we had to get people to understand that *black* jeans were now available. And more than just announcing that, the poster also needed to communicate something about the kind of person who would wear black jeans. We needed to make clear: You will be different. You won't be one of the crowd. You won't be one of the flock.

To reinforce the point we were making visually, we added a single line of text:

WHEN THE WORLD ZIGS, ZAG.

The client finally relented and ran the poster.

So successful was this piece of advertising that Levi's presented me with a life-size black sheep and we eventually adopted the black sheep as BBH's logo. Like any great logo, it represents far more than a memorable corporate identity. It's not only about standing out, being distinctive, and not following the crowd, it also drives our creative thinking and our values.

The black sheep became our identity *and* our philosophy. Even now in our creative briefs at BBH we always ask ourselves:

Where's the *zag* in our thinking?

By looking in the opposite direction, you might just find something new.

Storytelling

Storytelling is the most powerful form of communication ever invented. Through stories we learn, entertain, communicate, and socialize with each other.

You could argue that we're machines made specifically to tell stories. When we're telling a story in person everything about us is contributing to the power of that tale. Our very physicality helps deepen our and others' responses to it. And, of course, everybody can tell a story. We all do it every day. (Though some of us, as with creativity, are better at it than others.)

Why is storytelling so important to the creative process?

Well, it's what we build our ideas around. It's the very fabric of our thoughts. If the idea is the foundation of the creative process, then the story is the vehicle that delivers it, making it memorable and provocative.

Even an architect constructing a building is ultimately telling a story – a story of why and how. Think of Richard Rogers and Renzo Piano's Centre Pompidou in Paris. Its striking architecture encourages you to question and think creatively before you've even stepped over the threshold. By turning the building inside out, they challenged others' perceptions of just what a building *should* look like.

A story always leaves you feeling something. And despite all our advances, all our supposed sophistication, listening to a great story, told brilliantly, still enthralls us the most.

Technology

Right now we live in a world exploding with new and exciting technological developments. The digital revolution is transforming industries, re-imagining careers, and changing forever the way we create and do things.

So it's understandable that sometimes we forget technology should be the handmaiden of our creativity.

Needs no batteries, wires or chargers.
Easy to use.
Transportable.
Doesn't activate airport security.
Works anywhere.
Cheap.

But this forgetfulness can lead to two dangers:

We become in awe of technology.
We fear technology.

We must always remember technology is not an idea. It's the means to *express* an idea. So under no circumstances should you become overawed by it.

New technologies have been coming and going forever. And, historically, when a new technology develops we're often not quite sure how best to use it. There is for a time what I like to call a creative deficit.

Gutenberg may have invented the printing press and movable type, but he didn't create the publishing industry.

The Lumière Brothers may have invented the motion-picture camera, but they didn't invent the movie industry.

It was creative people – those storytellers I just mentioned – who realized the potential of these new technologies and dreamed up the groundbreaking, imaginative ways to harness them.

So it is with digital technology. We need our very best creative people exploring how we can most intriguingly communicate ideas through this ever-evolving medium.

Which leads me to my second point.

Don't be afraid of technology.

Many creative types resist new technologies, despite the fact this means missing out on new ways of self-expression. This is probably because we're all so superstitious. We're not sure where our own creativity comes from so therefore we resist change altogether.

My advice?

Relax. Don't worry about it but don't ignore it either. Embrace it as an excuse to play around with something new. You may soon find yourself having a lot of fun.

Without technology, our creativity would be limited to singing each other a song, telling stories, or scratching drawings on a cave wall. And as wonderful as all these activities are, you have to admit they're a bit limiting.

Just remember that no matter what piece of technology has been invented, from the camera to the computer, or will be invented, and no matter what value it claims to deliver, if it can't in some shape or another deliver the full impact of a well-told story its worth will eventually diminish.

Cynicism

Cynicism is the death of creativity. It will kill an idea and a creative career faster and more completely than anything else.

By and large, creativity is a positive act, a force for good, and it challenges us to change, not least so that we can see the world in a different, hopefully more interesting way.

Creativity should encourage, enthuse, engage, and entertain.

Always remember an idea is a precious gift and easy to destroy. If you fall prey to cynicism, doubt and disbelief will soon infect your thinking and your work.

A cynic might sound smart, sometimes even witty, but rarely are they productive. So surround yourself with positivity and possibility. With people who challenge and question. And as soon as anyone resorts to cynicism, move on.

I like this quote by the American writer and satirist H. L. Mencken:

A cynic is a man who, when he smells flowers, looks around for a coffin.

So be careful. Don't surround yourself with people who want to bury your ideas.

'Why' is the most important word you'll ever use.

Creativity is all about exploration and going where no one has gone before. Just like an explorer, you're hoping to head into uncharted territories.

Asking 'Why?' is the key to starting that journey.

Now some people are going to find your asking 'Why?' all the time incredibly aggravating. Same as we all feel when a child asks 'Why?' again and again. *You* will even feel a little childish.

Keep asking the question.

The greatest creative people are great precisely because they hold on to a childlike simplicity and urge to question everything. This is sometimes referred to as creative ignorance, not just the rejection of accepted practices but a complete ignorance of them. It's the creatives who challenge accepted ways of thinking, consciously or unconsciously, that end up making the very best work.

So ask 'Why?' of everyone and everything. With this one simple question you'll be on the path to discovering an idea that challenges the world, an idea that gets everyone talking.

Pre/Occupation

Creativity isn't an occupation; it's a preoccupation.

The truly great creative people I know are constantly working. Looking, thinking, watching. They are curious by nature, fascinated not just by their own interests and experiences but those of other people too. *Everything* they encounter is being absorbed, processed, and re-formed, eventually to return in some new shape as an idea. I think of these people as transmitters – they absorb diverse, random messages, influences, and thoughts, then reinterpret and play them back to an audience in new and fresh ways.

Being fascinated, inquisitive, informed, and engaged is an all-day, everyday activity. It doesn't have an on-off button. It doesn't have a stopwatch attached. It is constant. A way of living and of being that never switches off. If you don't want to live like that then don't follow a creative profession.

Of course, the danger is that your passion spills over into obsession and you become a bore. Nobody wants to be one of those.

So be careful.

I work in advertising but I don't live in it.

And neither should you. You really ought to get out more often. Look around you. The more surprising and disparate your inputs are, the more interesting the outcomes will be.

Staying open to new ideas, new places, and new people will feed your creative soul. Lack of inspiration may be just another way of saying lack of experience.

Philosophy

I define creativity as 'the expression of self.'

> The greatest creative practitioners put a little bit of themselves into their work. Their beliefs, concerns, and ambitions.

> So too your work should be an accumulation of your beliefs, personality, and experiences. Of course, if you're working in the applied arts collaborating with a client has its challenges, but even so you need to set out some guiding principles.

So ask yourself:

> *What excites me?*
> *What drives me?*

Fail to figure out the answers to these questions and your work will be empty.

> For me, it is all about irreverence and its power to challenge and question. Irreverence drives the work I like and the work I want to create. I believe it gives my creativity an energy and attention that makes it stand out. And getting noticed is a prerequisite of any good idea.

The danger is that irreverence can be too challenging. So that's where humor comes in. If you express your irreverent idea with wit and a smile, you'll soon find your audience much more accepting.

Now I don't want you to panic at the thought that you've got to get a philosophy by lunchtime. And don't Google 'philosophy' to see what comes up. Just be aware that you need to develop one. I just let my philosophy emerge. My work and the work I like gave me the answer.

Ultimately, if you don't have a guiding philosophy underpinning your thinking and work then what you produce won't touch people. It can't. And that's the most important task of any piece of creativity.

Remove Your Headphones

Do you know what really upsets me?
(Apart from peanut butter.)

When I see one of my creatives wandering through their day with headphones on. Why are they cutting themselves off from the world?

Inspiration is all around us. All that we see, hear, touch, taste, and smell helps us to form new ideas, even if we don't always realize it.

So why reduce the amount of inspiration reaching you?
Why wear headphones?

To be a successful creative person you have to be fascinated by the world and all its wonders, absurdities, failings, and mishaps. The world can be a constant source of inspiration but you must absorb it through *all* your senses before you can hope to channel it into fresh ideas.

Without inspiration, our creativity dries up and we start repeating ourselves.

The fashion designer Paul Smith told me a great
story that demonstrates how you can find inspiration
just about anywhere and when you least expect it.

He was in Milan and his flight back to the UK had been
delayed. Instead of sitting down, plugging in his
headphones, and unplugging his brain, he decided
to go for a walk.

As he walked along, something caught his eye
on the ground – a little lucky charm that had fallen
off a bracelet. In a flash of inspiration, he thought it
would make a great button for a shirt.

Some thirty thousand shirts later, that simple flash
of inspiration proved to be right.

So take off your headphones and let the world in.

You'll be amazed at how many free ideas are out there.

Mix with the Best

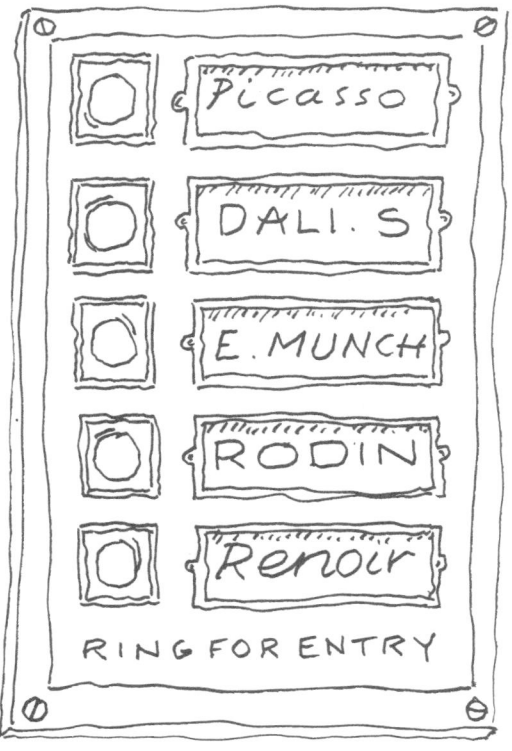

There's a well-known saying that goes like this:

Read shit and you'll think shit and you'll create shit.

Now if you aspire to shit then that's what you should do.
But I have a funny feeling you don't.

There's no doubt you get better when you surround yourself with great things and great people. And that holds true in whatever field you're in. Talent rubs off. Just like in sport – the more you play with better players, the better you become. For writers, painters, architects, designers, the same applies. This could be why galleries and museums are always so crowded with people. In the UK, more people now visit art galleries and museums on the weekend than go to football matches. Maybe that's why the British creative economy is doing so well whereas the last time the UK won the World Cup was 1966.

I know some people claim to do their best thinking on the toilet but I'm sure that's got more to do with relaxation than it has to do with bodily functions.

Whatever we do, we're always looking for inspiration. And inspiration, as I've said, can come from anywhere. But when we're looking at other creative work we need it to be great; greatness is what spurs us on.

It's also why we have to seek out inspiring creative environments to work. We constantly need to be pushed, challenged, even frightened into making our work better. There's no shame in admitting this.

It's said Jack Kerouac wrote his novel *On the Road* on a roll of toilet paper.*

It changed the course of the modern novel.

Toilet paper or not, it certainly wasn't crap.

* *It was actually a roll of Teletype paper, but never mind...*

Read The Economist

No, this book is not being sponsored in part or in any other way by that distinguished magazine.

So why am I suggesting you read it?

Well, for a number of reasons. First, it's important to consume information from unusual sources. We're always looking for inspiration, right? Well, if you only read creative journals, only visit the popular art galleries, and only see the same films, plays, and performances as everyone else, you'll soon start thinking like everyone else.

I'm not saying don't go out and do those things.
Please do. In fact, I'm imploring you to do so.

But what I'd like you to do is *flavor* those experiences with something else. Something different and unexpected. Something that expands your knowledge and appreciation of other types of creativity.

In the end, everything is connected and the more connections you make the more interesting your work will become. Being fascinated by everything is a surefire way to feed the creative soul – even if that means reading a magazine dedicated to economics. Which incidentally I would argue is more of an art than a science.

My next canvas depicts the repealing of the Glass-Steagall act!

There is a second reason for reading *The Economist*. One day you may find yourself commissioned by a financial company, business, or enterprise to create a campaign or design for them. When it comes time to pitch, you'll be amazed by how powerful your persuasion skills have become simply because you understand a little more about the field and what drives it.

It's no good having great ideas if you can't sell them.

More on that later.

Respect Don't Revere

Respect *don't* **revere.**

Putting anyone on a pedestal is dangerous. It implies they're better than everyone else. But they're not. We're all stepping-stones for the next generation.

> **Revere anyone or any one thing at your own risk. Doing so will over influence your work and impede your creativity. It will lead to imitation, not creation.**

Yes, it's important to learn from those who've gone before. I've only just said that great work and great creators are the greatest of teachers. But it's important that your admiration for others' work doesn't crowd out your own creativity.

> I've subtitled this book *There Are No Rules*. And genuinely there are none. Experiences, practices, philosophies, whatever you want to call them? Yes. But rules? No.

To create great work you should be making up your own beliefs as you go along, changing them one day to the next, always pushing against the boundaries of current thinking, trying to escape the confines of conventional wisdom. Resist the pressure to conform and your work will be anything but imitative.

Every generation has to push the boundaries of creativity forward. And to do that, you must believe in yourself and your vision. You must dare to be different. Revering your predecessors will put a stop to that.

So, do respect what's gone before. But revere it? Never.

Good Is the Enemy of Great

Good is the enemy of great.

Understand this and you'll be very successful.

At first reading it sounds absurd. How can this be?
Surely creativity is a progression. You go from
ordinary to OK to good and then on to great.
It's a simple progression, right?

I've had this great idea!

To some extent that's true. But more often than not coming up with a great idea is a rollercoaster ride of thoughts with no logical progression. You lurch from the interesting to the absurd to the good then back again to the absurd.

Within this maelstrom of thoughts veering all over the place, it can be easy to settle on something that feels right. Something that seems to make sense of all the confusion. You'll feel relief when you get to this point. You'll think you've cracked it. You'll feel good.

But then you have to take a step back from what feels really good and ask:

But is it great?

Great and idea Simpkins are 2 words that ravely go together!

And that is the hardest thing to do.

Because you're at good!

And your brain is saying surely this is great.

But your heart knows it isn't.

So park that good idea and keep going. Trust in inspiration to come up with a great idea – that idea that's going to put everything else in the shade.

Getting to good is hard enough, but given half the chance good will stop you from getting to great.

Whenever I show someone an idea and they say, *Oh, that's really good,* **I know I've got to tear it up, head back to the drawing board, and keep going.**

Persuasion

I can assure you Willoughby, that doesn't work. The idea's still crap!

Persuasion has a bad reputation because it's associated with selling things to people, sometimes selling them things they don't even want.

Shocking. Who would do such a thing?

The reality is that most of us spend a lot of time trying to persuade others, whether it's asking your child to eat their greens, explaining to colleagues why your football team is better than their team, or justifying why that Chanel dress you've just bought is really worth every penny you spent on it.

Overtly or otherwise, we're all trying to persuade. And just as virtually every conversational exchange involves persuasion, so it is with creativity. Yet mention the role of persuasion in creative work and just wait for the fireworks...

Nonetheless, persuasion can be a tool for good. When the artist Goya depicted the barbarities of the Napoleonic Wars in Spain, for example, he was making a powerful anti-war statement. He was also employing persuasion.

Specialize

Too many creative people think they don't need to specialize, that they can have lots of ideas on lots of different subjects all of which are going to be great. Wonderful as that would be, it's likely to result in disappointment. Yes, I know Leonardo da Vinci did it all – a great artist *and* a pioneering inventor whose inquiring mind stretched far and wide.

If you think you're the next Leonardo, fine. But I seriously doubt you are. It's been five hundred years since he dazzled the world with his genius and I can assure you I'm not holding my breath that you're next.

Having the courage and determination to focus on one subject or area of expertise gives you the solid foundation that is absolutely necessary if you're to come up with a truly great idea, one that will be key to your future success.

Once you've mastered one art form by all means have a go at another. Experimenting and playing at other means of expression can be very therapeutic. It can energize your creative thinking and there's nothing wrong with that.

But constantly chopping and changing your specialty will hinder your success.

Keep your focus!

Throughout my career I've worked with some wonderfully creative people but the most interesting conversations I've ever had are always with specialists – filmmakers, illustrators, designers, whatever. These are people who have specialized and stayed focused day in, day out. They have committed themselves fully to their chosen art form and that makes their work so much more special.

If you want to produce special work, it's worth collaborating with special people.

Practice
Makes Perfect

I remember many years ago talking to a steel engraver who created the illustration plates for newspapers. In those days, you were apprenticed to a master engraver for five years. Only after that were you qualified for the job. The first eighteen months of the apprenticeship were spent drawing straight lines. Once you'd mastered this, you could then move on to perspective.

Now I'm not suggesting you need to be quite so rigorous in your training. God forbid straight lines for eighteen months! But that dedication to perfection is essential to mastering your craft.

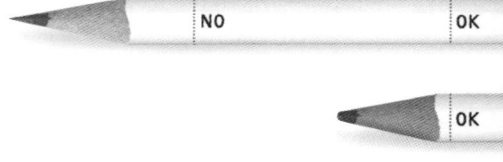

In his brilliant book *Outliers*, Malcolm Gladwell sets out the 10,000-hour rule. He worked out that to be good, really good, at something you need to put in at least 10,000 hours of practice. That might seem a bit daunting. And maybe it's only 9,500 hours. But remember, practice should be enjoyable too.

Now, as you know from the title of my book, I don't believe in rules. But I do believe in experience. And my experience tells me he's on to something.

As important as practice is, there's no point in constantly practicing unless you're perfecting whatever it is that you're working on.

Practice only makes perfect if you make progress.

GOOD   GREAT

GOOD   GREAT

GOOD   GREAT

GREAT

When to Turn Over the Page

I was at art school in a life-drawing class. The teacher was wandering around stopping at various easels, guiding, and advising us. He arrived at one student's easel and stopped the whole class before addressing us. He said:

When a drawing's going wrong, what you don't do is turn over the page and start again. You keep working on that drawing until it's right. Only then do you turn the page over. That's how you learn.

He then paused and added:

I suppose I'm talking about life as well.

This brilliant piece of advice about art and life has stayed with me throughout my career. Never move on until you've achieved what you set out to achieve. Keep working on something until you've got it right.

I remember listening to a radio interview with the British artist and sculptor Henry Moore on his eightieth birthday. The interviewer was naturally being effusive and overly flattering – or at least Moore thought so. He interrupted the interviewer to say that when he left the Royal College of Art there were about thirty other great sculptors. After forty years, there were just ten. And after sixty years, just three. His point was less that he was a genius and more that he kept at it, getting better and better as time went on. Persistence pays off.

Now, I happen to think Moore *was* a genius. But his point was well made. Unless you stick at it – whatever the 'it' is – you'll never know how good you can be. You can bet Moore never turned over the metaphorical page before he was good and ready.

Collaboration

Much today is written about collaboration and the need to work or brainstorm with others in order to bring an idea to fruition.

It's all very friendly and inclusive but be careful: Collaboration can easily turn into consensus.

Which rapidly becomes ordinary. Sitting around on beanbags holding hands and having a happy-clappy meeting will not lead to greatness.

Some people believe you can create brilliance by brainstorming with lots of people.

Well, you can't.

Collaboration is great for sex but not for creativity.

NOT THERE!

OOPS!

IS THAT YOURS?

SORRY!

IT'S NOT WORKING!

PUT IT WHERE

It's a bit like an orgy. Too many people makes for bad sex.

Another fine example of less is more.

How much collaboration is necessary and when you should collaborate does depend quite a lot on what it is you're creating. If you're a painter working on a canvas there will probably be no need to ask for a second opinion. I don't think Picasso had someone advising him where to put the eyes on his portraits of Dora Maar. But when Frank Gehry was designing the now-famous Guggenheim Museum in Bilbao, Spain, there was probably quite a lot of collaboration. Here's the important point though: Even if there was, every project still needs someone in charge with a crystal-clear vision. A creator with the big idea in their head. And so it was with Gehry. He alone came up with the idea for this stand-out, world-famous work of architecture. Once he had that idea in place, I'm sure he then worked closely with a team of architects and structural engineers to realize his vision.

No matter what you're creating, a single vision is fundamentally important. It is the driving force of any project. Whether you're working on a simple illustration or a vast building, understanding when and how you should collaborate will determine the success of your project.

The old saying that no one ever erected a monument to a committee is absolutely true. If you want to have an average idea then the group brainstorm is probably a good place to start. But who's interested in average?

Two's Company

There are exceptions to the single vision of creativity.

Remember, there are no rules!

One of the great traditions of the advertising industry and, indeed, many others is the practice of working in pairs – two minds coming together to solve a problem, write a script, compose music, etc. Think of Rodgers and Hammerstein, Lennon and McCartney, Dolce and Gabbana.

Because remember, you can't be good at everything. So the skill is to work with someone who is good at what you are not. That's why Renzo Piano worked with Richard Rogers, and Keith Richards works with Mick Jagger.

This can be a fun way to work. Bouncing ideas off each other, using the relationship to test outrageous thoughts, challenging each other to do better, dream bigger.

For this partnership to be effective, it's important that you come from opposing disciplines. You can't just be echoes of each other. You each need to bring something different to the party.

The Perfect team.

In advertising, the best partnerships are usually those formed between art director and writer. The reason for this is in their job titles: Art directors think visually; writers think in terms of narrative. I'm generalizing here, but what's important is that their starting points are different. And when these differences rub up against one another they will hopefully produce sparks. And it's these sparks that just might ignite an idea worth having.

Being like-minded is wonderful, and nodding in harmony is fine when listening to a piece of music – but *not* when generating a brilliant idea.

Reflection

I'm not talking about what you see in a mirror.

I'm talking about the ability to stand back from
what you've created and assess its worth.

Why is this important?

Creativity isn't an objective pursuit. Its value can't be
measured the way other skills can be. Does a vaccine
work? Will that iron girder support that building?
These questions have right and wrong answers,
whereas creativity is more often than not subjective.

Eventually, of course, its value will be confirmed, but
often long after it was created. Van Gogh was only able
to sell one of his paintings during his lifetime. And that
was to his brother. Now they sell for millions.

Assessing the value of what you're producing
while you're producing it has to be conducted with
different criteria. And by their very nature, these
will be highly personal.

Snap judgments and rapid decisions often lead to poor work. The ability to stand back from your thinking and give it what we call 'the overnight test' is essential. Unfortunately, we live in a world today that too often doesn't allow this.

'I want it now.'
'Tomorrow is too late.'

Time may be one of creativity's best friends, yet no one will give you any. You have to earn it.

To gauge if your idea will stand up to scrutiny necessitates reflection. Thanks to digital technology everything in this world has sped up drastically but that only makes it all that much more important to slow it down.

Our brains still operate in an analog world.

Bad Weather

There's no doubt creativity flourishes in adversity. Make things too comfortable and the creative juices stop flowing. We can all imagine the poor, starving artist working relentlessly in their attic studio, painting away until they drop. And while I'm not suggesting starving yourself is the best spur to great thinking, I do believe one discomfort is worthwhile:

Bad weather.

Why?
Because bad weather is generally great for ideas.

Now I've got nothing against sunny locales. Sydney, for instance, is one of my favorite cities. But it's not, in my view, a creative center.

We'll see prolonged outbreaks of genius over most of the country. Whilst London will suffer a severe drought of inspiration, followed by a crisis of confidence!

The problem with Sydney is its weather. It's just *too* good. If you're working in Sydney and struggling with a creative problem, all you have to do is look out the window, see the sun shining, and soon enough you'll hear the beckoning call of a couple of ice-cold beers waiting for you at that beachside bar down the street.

And what are you doing to do?
I think we all know the answer to that.

Great weather is probably why Hollywood turns out some truly awful movies. Who wants to labor over a cliché-ridden script in an effort to turn it into an Oscar-winner when you could be down by the pool at the Sunset Marquis? Sunny weather is great for shooting films but not so wonderful for writing them.

In comparison, London always ranks as one of the world's great creative centers.

Why? Because the weather is shit.

Rain is London's creative trump card. Want to go for a barbecue? Forget it. Every summer thousands of barbecues are sold and every year they rust away unused, ending up as landfill.

So wherever you're working, check the forecast. If you're getting too much sunshine and not enough rainfall, move somewhere where the weather is bad. Really bad.

It's amazing what it will do to get your creative juices going.

Ego

To any creative person, ego is both friend and foe.

> Ego is defined as the 'I' or 'the self.' And if creativity
> can be defined as the expression of self, it's no wonder
> why having a healthy ego is so important. Belief in what
> you're doing is fundamental.

**If you're truly great you're going to be creating
work that breaks barriers, changes the way we see
things, and alters our visual landscape.**

I can't possibly start the meeting. I'm waiting for my ego to arrive!

Leonardo's *Mona Lisa* changed the way we thought of portrait painting. On top of the incredible luminosity of his subject's skin, he painted her looking straight at you, confronting the viewer in a unique and profound way. Leonardo's conviction that a portrait could and should be painted differently helped make it one of the most famous in the world.

But too much ego can be your downfall. And that's called egotism. Losing touch with your audience and driving your thinking into a cul-de-sac.

Walking this fine line is difficult. How do we know when we've gone from the positive to the negative? From ego to egotism?

My simple test is when one of my creative colleagues starts to tell me everything they have done is brilliant. They replace ego with arrogance. That's when it all starts to go wrong.

Hubris

Creativity is one of the most unforgiving of careers. It's brutal. It rewards without question and it punishes remorselessly. It doesn't take prisoners and it has no respect for reputation. And the longer you go on doing it, the harder it gets. How many creative careers have we seen soar to great heights and then crash and burn? Brilliant one minute, tragic and vulnerable the next.

Hubris is one of creativity's great enemies and the natural consequence of egotism. Where hubris does differ, however, is in its absolute belief in itself, its total arrogance.

If Ego is all about the 'I,' hubris is all about the 'Me.'
An absolute belief in one's own genius.

Of course, you have to believe in what you're doing but
like everything in life excessive belief will destroy you.
One way to guard against this is to find a voice you can
trust. Someone who you can turn to who will tell you
the genuine truth.

The problem is your success will isolate you from
these voices. Without realizing it you will have become
surrounded by people who agree with everything you
suggest. Your youthful, insightful intuition will be
replaced by faded, clichéd renditions that carry echoes
of greatness but sadly not the intensity.

**To be truly great you have to listen, you have
to understand humility, and you have to recognize
your own vulnerability. And that, I can assure
you, is hard.**

Yes, it seems to capture
something elusive about me!

Editing

Anyone can have an idea. In fact, lots of people find it easy to have lots of ideas. The secret is in identifying which ideas are great and which ideas are just the outpourings of a deranged mind.

This is where editing becomes important.

Editing is not only about ensuring the idea you're working on isn't weighed down by unnecessary complexity but also that you're working on the right idea.

Spotting the right idea is as important as having it.

I've known creative people who could spew out ideas endlessly. The problem was that often they had no idea which ones were great and which were completely useless.

That's why earlier I recommended teaming up with someone who you trust and can creatively rely on. In this relationship you will become editors for each other.

**In creative work it really is hard to be both
subjective and objective. A great idea comes from
a subjective point of view but then it has to be
reviewed objectively to see whether or not it will
work. This second objective stage is called editing.**

Editing isn't just about taking things out; it's also about
understanding what has value and how that value can
be amplified. In art galleries this is called curating: The
process of working out in what order the works should
be shown, what should be highlighted, and what should
be left out.

Don't Second-Guess

Many people believe that the more you know about your audience, the better your work will be. This is why in certain creative industries market research is so prevalent. The movie industry and advertising in particular are stuck in the headlights of this dark art.

Henry Ford was famously quoted as saying:

> *If I'd asked people what they wanted, they would have said faster horses.*

Instead, he came up with a motor car they could afford.

I know what you're thinking!

Consensus leads to predictability. A great creative work surprises its audience by presenting ideas and thoughts never encountered before. That's the thrill of a memorable idea.

When Matt Groening created *The Simpsons***, he wasn't responding to a piece of market research about dysfunctional families. He just thought this particular family would be a great vehicle for observing the world we live in.**

Inspiring people isn't a mathematical process. You've got to surprise yourself as well as your audience. There is a randomness to creating that must be celebrated not scorned. If you look up the word 'surprise' in the dictionary, you'll notice that nowhere does it say, 'as expected.'

Beware of Fashion

We are living in a world increasingly driven by fashion. From the food we eat to where we live to the car we drive, fashion informs our decision-making processes more and more. Why is this?

I suppose because in the 'developed world' at least most of our needs are so well supplied that we now take functionality for granted. Cars, for instance, don't break down anymore. And when was the last time you called a TV-repairman or took your trainers to be repaired?

When assessing whether or not to buy something, we now tend to assume – or ignore entirely – functionality, concentrating instead on making the right fashion statement.

We want our decisions, especially our purchasing decisions, to say to the world out there: Look at me – I'm forward-looking, modern, aware, connected to what's going on. Buying into what's fashionable is the quickest way to communicate this.

But the danger in dabbling with what's fashionable *when creating* is that you'll get it wrong, or that by the time you've executed your work the world will have moved on.

For this reason, chasing fashion for its own sake is bound to end in failure.

So what should you be doing? The answer to that is innovating. By doing something different, by not following the crowd, you'll instead *lead* fashion. And, incidentally, dictating to the world just what is and isn't fashionable is a hell of a lot of fun.

This is what James Dyson accomplished when he developed the technology for his bag-less vacuum cleaner. Not only did he innovate the way a vacuum works, but, driven by innovation, he also changed the way it looked. And in the end created a must-have consumer product.

If you think about it, making a vacuum cleaner fashionable could quite possibly be the ultimate creative achievement.

Something tells me, 20 years from now you'll regret those trousers!

Timing

This is one of those impossible debates.

Timing, they say, is everything.

A brilliant idea at the wrong time will fail.
(People who work in the fashion industry
understand this better than anyone.)

But the question is: If your idea is *truly* brilliant can
it overcome this issue?

Naturally it depends where and how your creativity
is being used. If you're Jonathan Ive, chief designer
at Apple, your creativity is driven by technology,
and success therefore comes from finding creative
solutions to technological innovation. Whereas
if you're a screenwriter in the film industry, success
will depend on the brilliance of your script *and* whether
you've caught a wave.

Of course, no one knows if they've got the timing just
right in advance, but asking certain questions can help.
So ask yourself:

Have I got my finger on the pulse of what's going on?
Will this idea inspire people to follow me?
Is my idea daring or challenging?
Does it touch a truth?
Will it capture people's attention and make headlines?
Is it fresh?

**I've asked similar questions throughout this book.
And I will carry on asking them. They are key to
initiating and inspiring creativity.**

A great idea creates its own timing. And that's
what you should be searching for. By being tuned in,
aware, sensitive to what is going on, and by keeping
an open mind, you can create the circumstances
to make that happen.

You can make your own timing.

The other point is to stop worrying about it.

You'll never be able to predict the future so stop trying.

On my tombstone I'm going to have the following
words carved:

Presentation

Selling is one of the most undervalued skills of any creative career.

In a perfect world, everyone would instantly recognize genius and no artist would need to sell their vision or work. Now I know this may come as a bit of a blow, but it's not a perfect world. And the fact that it isn't is in a way a spur to your creativity. But that's a slightly different point.

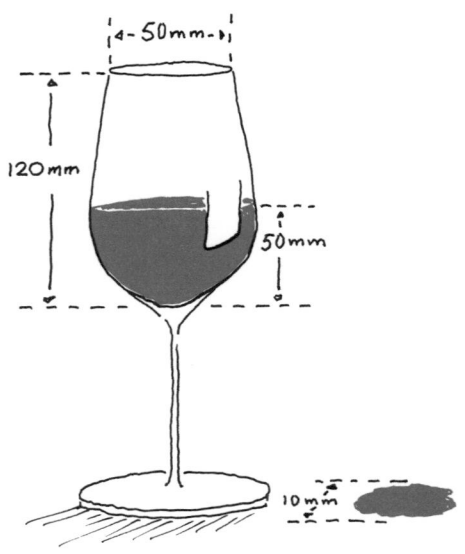

The ability to sell a good idea is almost as important as having one. Capturing the essence of your work in one succinct sound bite is crucial to encouraging the person buying it and to helping the public understand it. Cubism, Surrealism, Pop Art, such labels are all attempts to capture the essence of an art movement and to help the public access and appreciate the many different works each one encompasses.

A great idea is only a great idea when you've shared it with the world. And to do that effectively you need to be able to define what it is you've created.

In the commercial world, this is called pitching an idea and mastering this art is essential. To an editor with a book to sell, a producer with a TV show to option, whatever, a strong and arresting presentation can be the difference between success and rejection.

When pitching an idea it's important to keep it simple. Your goal should be to get the idea to open out inside the head of the person you're pitching to. If brevity is the soul of wit, so it is with a successful pitch.

Of course, you can always leave behind a body of work to be discovered after your death. But that's not really all that satisfying. Sadly for many great artists their genius was only recognized after their death. It may sound flippant but had they been a bit better at presenting, perhaps a few more of their groundbreaking works would have been recognized in their lifetimes.

The Power of Fame

Fame has its own power.

But I don't mean the power of *your* fame. I mean the power of your *work's* fame.

> **Great creativity has a life beyond the confines of the audience it was originally conceived for. It becomes iconic. Instantly recognizable and powerfully influential. In reaching this status it becomes the benchmark for everything else that follows, rewriting the way the world looks at things.**

Think of Apple's iPhone, Frank Lloyd Wright's Fallingwater or Le Corbusier's LC2 armchair. These creations changed industries and inspired lifestyles. They achieved fame and recognition and came to be revered throughout the world.

Regarding your role as the new Bond villain The ears will have to go!

How did they do that?

By challenging the conventional, daring to be different, and anticipating future changes in behavior. Their creators didn't compromise on their ideas or in the execution of those ideas. They believed in their vision and pursued it relentlessly.

Everything I've written so far in this book is an attempt to show how *your* creativity can achieve this status. But do be careful – as valuable as fame is, it can also be a trap.

You see, once fame is achieved, your audience will begin to expect you to do more of the same, making it more difficult for you to step out of the shadows of your own creation and produce something different. This is a particular problem for actors. Being typecast in one role might be good for a time but it soon becomes a burden. Actors have to have the courage to break free.

Have you that courage?
Will your audience accept your new vision?
If you don't try, you'll never know.

Failures

Many people talk about failures as opportunities to learn. Saying this seems to make people feel wise and worldly.

Well, I say bollocks to failure.

Don't dwell on it.

Move on.

Forget it.

If you're genuinely creative and trying to create work that hasn't been seen before, that is really fresh, then you will have to contend with other peoples' doubts. All too often your idea will be greeted with 'Oh, that's really different...' or 'I haven't seen that before.'

Of course, it's different.
That's what makes it great.

Here's the problem with dwelling on past failures: When faced with these doubting voices, suddenly you too will start to doubt your idea. You will start to think, 'Perhaps, they're right. Perhaps, this *isn't* as great as I thought it was. Perhaps, I *should* do something that's more familiar...'

NO! NO! NO!

Chances are that your idea does not work. But even so that's the risk you have to take if you want to create great work. Being ordinary is easy. The world's full of people who can do ordinary.

So if you haven't failed, you haven't really tried.

Plan on failing. But when you do, don't dwell on it.

Money, Money, Money

Money's the last reason for doing anything!

That's what you said last time I ASKED for a raise!

Too many creative careers have been destroyed because money was chased, not opportunity.

Creativity has to be nurtured, cared for, invested in. Money just wants to exploit your career, without any concern for its longevity or future.

Of course, money is important and oils a lot of wheels. It pays the mortgage and it can buy freedom.

But it's important to remember that if money has a voice, it doesn't have a soul. It's a tool not a philosophy.

If you plan to pursue a creative career (or I would argue any career), make money your sole objective at your own peril. More than likely, you'll end up with either a very short career or a very unsatisfactory one.

The best way to get rich – if that's what you want – is to invent something the world wants, admires, or talks about, something that will capture our imagination and make us feel better, emotionally or physically.

Creating something *you* love and that *you* would buy is the best way forward. Try to create with only money on your mind and you'll end up with a second-rate idea – and poor.

Don't Read About Yourself

CALL MY LAWYER! NOW! SUE! SHOCK! DISGUSTED!

THE DAILY SLANDER

I was given a wonderful piece of advice very early on in my career:

Don't read anything about yourself or your work in the press.

See, chances are that you've created something that is controversial and so some talentless critic has made disparaging comments about it.

Why would they do that?

Unfortunately, it is easier to knock something than to praise it. Critics think it makes them look smart and the news outlets believe that kind of criticism sells more copies (or, these days, clicks, tweets, etc.).

The best and only response is this: **Ignore it.**

There's nothing more annoying for a critic then to know that you can't be bothered with their nonsense. With critics (as with cynics), don't give them the oxygen of more publicity. Because let's face it: Publicity is all they're after. And as a bonus, by not reading the criticism, you won't get upset and expend valuable energy on negativity.

Follow my advice and it's easy:

You win, they lose.

Craft

Six people tell the same joke, but only one of them makes you laugh.

Why?

Because that one individual understands the timing and rhythm that every story needs. And they know how to employ it.

That's craft.

Sadly we live in a world where the value of craft has been devalued. Technology allows us to do more things and to do them faster than ever before. But that doesn't mean that what we're producing is any better.

Doing something quickly is not the same as doing it well.

As I said ealier, technology may expand our capacity to express ourselves but it can also mask creativity. Talk to any sound engineer in a recording studio.

Understanding the craft of your chosen medium and understanding how to use it to best effect is fundamental to success. If creativity is 80% idea, it's also 80% execution. Respecting the balance between these two contradictory statements is crucial.

Valuing the craft of your chosen profession will be critical to your success.

Swap Seats

Routine stunts your creativity.

All too often in your creative life you will find yourself stuck. You'll be beating your brains out trying to think of something different but despite your best efforts nothing is happening. Inspiration will not strike.

Well, there's nothing unusual about this situation, so don't panic. I've found there's one simple trick you can use that will get you out of any creative rut.

Swap seats.

Human beings are creatures of habit and so much of what we do is programmed into us over time without our ever stopping to question it. Now, to a certain extent, a daily routine is essential. But if your job is to come up with new ideas – really fresh ones that capture our attention – it will pay to change your routine.

Say you're working in advertising. Think about how much of your and the team's behavior is governed by daily routine. You all come in each morning as usual, sit in your usual spots, and drink your usual cups of coffee – then you try and come up with an unusual idea.

*If each day is business as usual how can you possibly
create something unusual?*

Here's an easy first step to break the monotony: Switch
desks with a colleague. Suddenly, even though you've
only moved a few feet away, your perspective will have
changed and your brain will be looking at everything
from a different angle. And looking at things differently
jogs the imagination into action.

**If you want to take it a step further, change cities
or even better continents (but only to a place with
bad weather; see page 86). It's amazing what a
plane ticket can do for your creativity. When I went
to work in New York for two years, it was one of
the most stimulating periods of my career.**

Remember: Great work cannot be original, it can only
be fresh and the first step to creating fresh work can
be as simple as sitting somewhere different. Then,
at the least, you'll have a fresh perspective.

The McCartney Syndrome

It is said that most political careers end in disaster. It could also be said most creative careers end in clichés.

To constantly come up with challenging ideas is difficult at the best of times. But as your reputation grows in strength and notoriety so too will your desire to believe everything you do is genius.

I've sat in meetings with famous film directors discussing an idea and realized the executives they've brought along are only there to agree with them. Yet, as I've said elsewhere, honesty is at the core of outstanding creativity. Honesty in idea *and* assessment.

Great people need someone who will challenge their thinking, someone they can trust and respect.

Every McCartney needs a Lennon.

Sadly, Paul lost his Lennon and ended up writing 'Mull of Kintyre.' And this from a man who gave us 'Yesterday,' 'Eleanor Rigby,' and numerous other classics. So whatever happens, hold on to honesty. Hold on to your Lennon.

Think Short Term

People often ask me:
> *Do you have a five-year plan?*

To which I always reply:
> *No, I have a five-minute plan.*

**I know some people will say that's irresponsible
and to a certain extent they're right. But if you're
building a creative career you've got to be open
to the unexpected.**

As is often said, there are no facts on the future. So
stop trying to predict what's ahead of you and choose
instead to make this moment, the one you're living right
now, the most enjoyable and rewarding it can be.

I continually say to people, 'Do interesting things
and interesting things will happen to you.' Whenever
you plan your life you cut yourself off from those
opportunities that could be the most rewarding.

Creativity is about reinvention. And you can't reinvent
yourself if you've already decided what you're going to
be doing in five years time. In fact, knowing that is truly
depressing and will never lead to inspired thinking.

We all have to find our own ways of living in the
moment. Exploring it, expanding it, and indulging it.
That's why children are so wonderful. They live for each
moment and therefore get so much more out of life.

Predictions about the future are meaningless.
They rarely come true.

**The best way to predict the future is to invent
it. And that's done by making the present as
interesting as possible.**

Don't Get
Too Comfortable

I've got some bad news for you: There's a good chance that becoming successful will breed your failure. Bit of a bummer that, especially if you've just got used to turning left when boarding an airplane.

So if success can breed failure, how do you avoid this fate?

First of all, it's not a matter of shunning success. And I'm not suggesting the secret to being a successful artist or creative is to remain poor. What I am suggesting is that you watch out for comfort. For as you earn more and more money, that money will make you more and more comfortable. You can afford the bigger car, the bigger house, the bigger studio.

When you become successful, after a time holding on to the real world becomes increasingly difficult. People start calling you a genius and suddenly everything you've ever done is brilliant. You are blessed with the Midas touch.

Your success will, in fact, distance you from the very world that stimulated the ideas that made you successful. It will isolate you.

And isolation is bad for creativity. Success or no, you remain as vulnerable as the next person. Your so-called brilliance is built on your day-to-day experiences so be very wary about losing access to them. Real-life experiences feed a creative person's work and outlook.

The best creative people manage to keep a grip on reality whatever they achieve. And that can be as basic as knowing the price of a loaf of bread or a pint of milk. So beware the seduction of the chauffeur-driven lifestyle.

The Ten-Year Rule (And How to Avoid It)

Here's a hard thing to accept.

**The great work in most creative careers is made
within a span of ten years.**

Think about it. Whether it's musicians, artists,
filmmakers, or designers, it's always in a ten-year
period that they create their best, most outstanding
work, the work that will define and sustain their
career for the rest of their life. Once they've made
their breakthrough, established a genre, or made
their point of view easily recognizable, they are then
able to repeat what they've created.

Wherever you look in the creative world it's the same.
Mick Jagger can travel around the world singing
'Jumpin' Jack Flash' and twenty thousand people will
turn up and applaud him – over forty-five years after
he wrote it with Keith Richards. Or Lucian Freud who,
once he had established his reputation as the greatest
portrait painter of the late twentieth century, kept on
painting portraits for the rest of his life.

To keep repeating the same thing once you've achieved
greatness is perfectly acceptable with many art forms.
But for some, such as advertising, you will need to have
a new idea every day. And that idea can't be like the one
you had yesterday.

Constant innovation can be exhausting and it's one of the reasons why advertising is so often seen as a young person's industry. There aren't many seventy-five-year-old art directors in our business.

So, how do you avoid the ten-year rule and continue to create great creative work across a fifteen-, twenty-, or even thirty-year career?

Here are some simple answers, a summary in short of all that's come before:

Don't become a cynic.

Surround yourself with people who aren't afraid of challenging you.

Stay engaged and remain curious about the world.

And last, but not least (and perhaps the real reason why the ten-year rule kicks in once success has been achieved): Remember money isn't a philosophy, it's a tool. It's the last reason why you should do anything.

Fun

Have fun.

This could well be the most important tip to remember when pursuing a creative career. Unless you enjoy what you do you're never going to be great at it so make sure you're having fun too. Of course, enjoying yourself doesn't guarantee the work that results will be any good...

> Throughout this book, I've talked about fearlessness, heartache, anger, persistence. All of which don't sound like much fun. And you're right. Creativity is a mixture of many emotions – that image of the tortured artist comes to mind here.

But ultimately a creative career puts you in an incredibly privileged position. Expressing your ideas, pursuing your dreams, creating a legacy for others to follow and build on is exciting and daunting, yes, but also fun.

> Painting a picture, writing a story, composing a song, whatever creative activity you pursue, you'll be the one in charge. Where do you want to go with that story? Who's in it? Who falls in love? Who dies? How does it end? You decide.

There are no limits to one's imagination. Even when you find yourself working for a client who keeps saying no to your ideas. In that case, it's just up to you to convince that person your vision is worth it.

All this freedom can be incredibly liberating and exciting. When Irvine Sellar commissioned architect Renzo Piano to design the Shard in London, it is said Piano sketched out his vision on a napkin over lunch. You can't tell me he wasn't excited. He was. Sellar bought into that excitement and together they created one of Europe's tallest and most talked about buildings. Apparently Sellar has the napkin framed in his office.

Whatever you're doing, whatever difficulties you're encountering, remember how lucky you are and be sure to have fun.

Another thing to remember:
Humor is the antidote to authority.

Somewhere at some time we were brainwashed into thinking fun is bad and unthinkingly took on board the puritanical belief that we shouldn't be enjoying ourselves. This same thinking is common in totalitarian regimes. They don't like fun either.

I say screw 'em.

Let's strike a blow for freedom and creativity.

Enjoy yourself, express your ideas, and have fun doing so. You'll do whatever it is that much better.

Digest These Thoughts

I told you page 38 was hard to stomach!

Creativity should never be predictable. It should surprise, entertain and inspire. It should encourage you to look at the world in a fresh way. If possible, it should also be useful, so here's something you've never tried before:

EAT MY WORDS

If you've managed to get the special limited edition of this book, printed on edible paper with vegetable inks (organic, I hope), it will feed more than just your imagination.

It's a unique way of digesting thoughts... As long as they don't stick in your throat... OK, OK, that's enough of the clichés. I don't want to over cook this idea. Oops, sorry, slipped again!

Thanks to Chef Anna Hansen MBE of The Modern Pantry, the acclaimed London restaurant, we even have the perfect recipe for a quiet night in with your creative partner.

To discover the recipe and watch me and Anna cooking up a storm, search 'Hegarty on (Cooking) Creativity' on YouTube. Enjoy.

John Hegarty would like to thank Anna Hansen MBE for generously applying her culinary talents to cooking up the special edition of this book, Sid Russell for his usual brilliance and patience, and Chloe Woodman for her typing skills.

First published in the United Kingdom in 2014 by Thames & Hudson Ltd, 181A High Holborn, London WC1V 7QX

Hegarty on Creativity: There Are No Rules © 2014 John Hegarty
Illustrations (John calls them scribbles) © 2014 John Hegarty

Text pages designed by Fred Birdsall studio
Cover illustration by Paul Wearing

British Library Cataloguing-in-Publication Data
A catalogue record for this book is available from the British Library

ISBN 978-0-500-51724-6

Printed and bound in China by Everbest Printing Co. Ltd

To find out about all our publications, please visit **www.thamesandhudson.com** There you can subscribe to our e-newsletter, browse or download our current catalogue, and buy any titles that are in print.